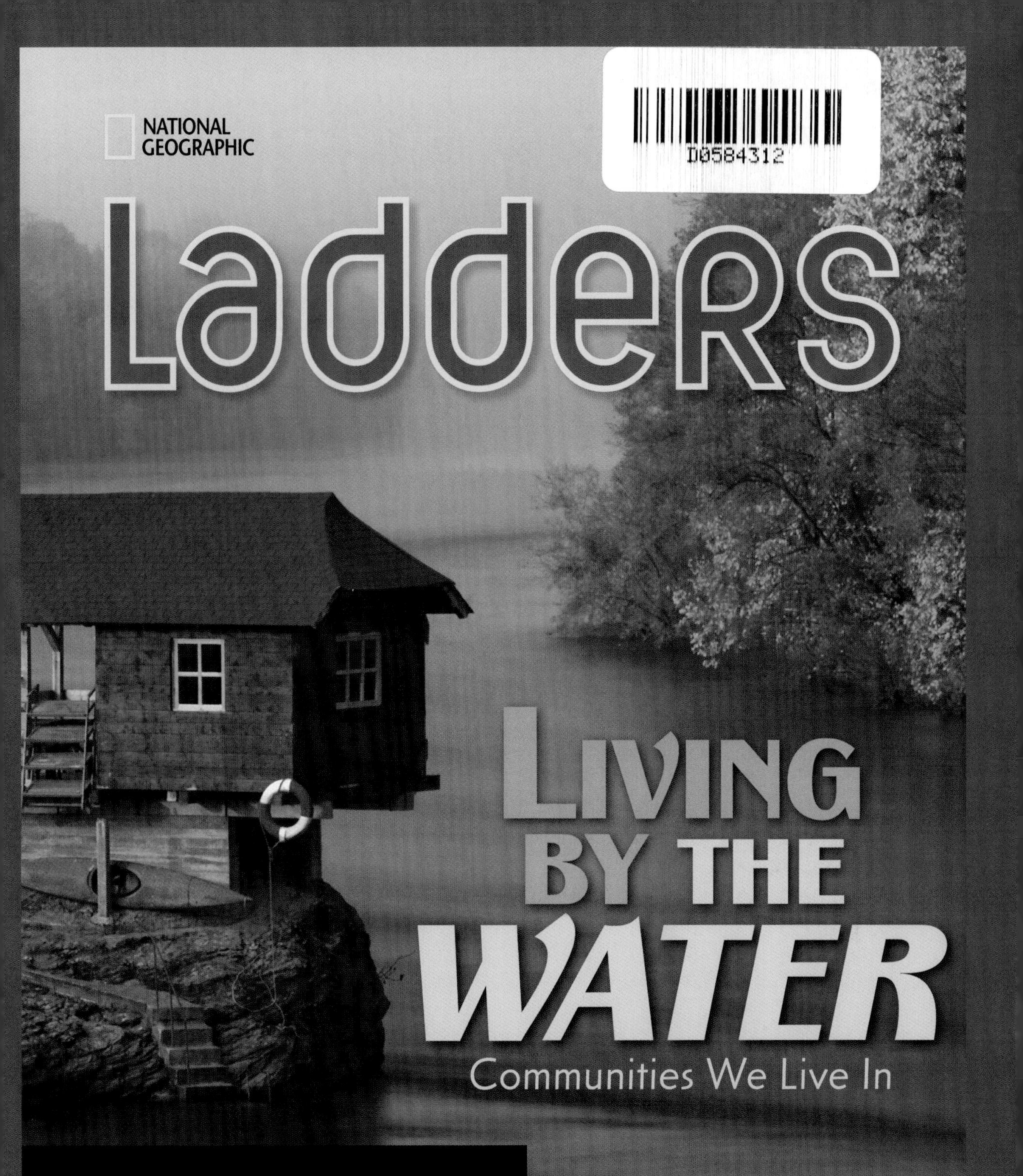

Living by the Water

Communities We Live In

GENRE Narrative

Read to find out about the Colorado River.

RESCUE A RIVER

by Becky Manfredini

Jon Waterman enters the headwaters of the Colorado River. He is in Rocky Mountain National Park in Colorado.

Jon Waterman and Pete McBride are writers and photographers. One day in 2008, they took a trip down the Colorado River. These men knew that farms and cities were taking lots of water from the river. Jon and Pete wanted to find out how this was affecting the river and the living things that need its water. They started their trip at the **headwaters**. That is the place where the river begins. It is high in the Colorado Mountains.

Jon spent 150 days paddling 1,450 miles. Pete joined Jon for parts of the trip. But Pete wanted to see the river from above, too. So he took pictures of it from a plane.

Jon and Pete saw different types of land. They saw the bright city of Las Vegas. They saw deserts and the Grand Canyon. But the land wasn't the only thing that changed. The river itself changed as it flowed to the sea.

Jon Waterman travels around the world. He writes about the ways people can protect our planet.

Pete McBride uses a special camera when he takes photographs from a raft. His cameras are sealed so that water cannot leak inside them.

THE MIGHTY COLORADO RIVER

For six million years, the Colorado River flowed through western lands. Plants and fish filled its waters. But more people began to live in the area. People needed more water from the river. Today, more than 30 million people depend on the Colorado River. They use its water for drinking and many other reasons. Farms use the most water. The river provides farms as far away as California with the water they need to grow crops.

Jon checks out smaller rivers that flow into the Colorado River. This is the Rio Hardy. The word *rio* means river in Spanish.

Jon and Pete watched the river from their rafts. They saw that the amount of water was getting lower. Less water is flowing through this river than just a few years ago. Some people worry about droughts, times of little or no rainfall. Droughts could dry up the river more. Many people depend on the Colorado River's water. Will there always be enough?

A DISAPPEARING RIVER

Jon and Pete paddled way down the Colorado River. Inside the country of Mexico, the river water turned into thick mud. Their rafts got stuck. The men had to push their rafts out with their paddles.

The men wondered how far the mud would go. Would it reach all the way to the river's **delta**? A delta is land built up by loose dirt carried by a river. Until 1998, the Colorado River flowed all the way to the Gulf of California. It flowed through a grassy delta before pouring into the gulf. This delta was once filled with birds and animals. Today,

it is much smaller than it was. The Colorado River is polluted and no longer flows all the way to the Gulf of California. Mud has replaced the flowing river. The animals that used to live there have gone away.

With all of the water gone, Jon and Pete had to carry their rafts on their backs. The men looked around. They couldn't help but worry. More than 300,000 birds stop along the river delta each year. They rest on their way to warmer places. But if the river delta is not cleaned up, the birds won't have a healthy place to rest in the future.

In Mexico, the once-clear water of the Colorado River is now muddy and filled with trash.

WHAT COMMUNITIES CAN DO

Jon and Pete took their trip for several reasons. One reason was to show how important the Colorado River is to animals. The men want to **conserve**, or protect, the river. People can conserve by using less water to grow crops and water lawns and keeping the river clean. Then plants and animals won't lose their homes. Jon and Pete are asking people to save the Colorado River.

The men's river journey also teaches how important rivers are to people. Rivers carry **fresh water** to farms, towns, and cities. Fresh water contains little salt. It is good for growing food, drinking, and washing. We need to make sure there will always be plenty of fresh water.

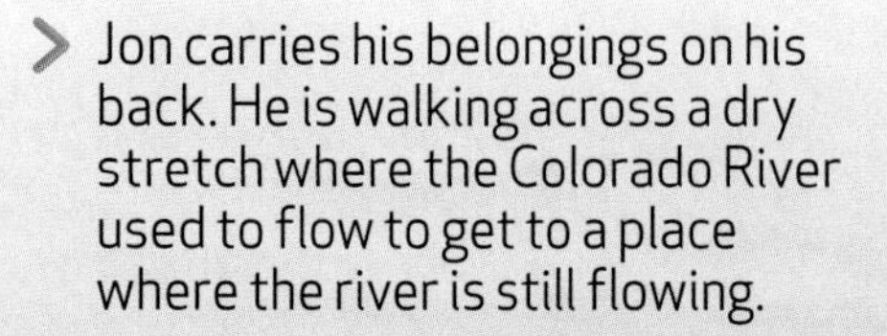

Jon carries his belongings on his back. He is walking across a dry stretch where the Colorado River used to flow to get to a place where the river is still flowing.

CONSERVE OUR PLANET'S FRESH WATER

Conserve water at home. Limit the use of tap water for showers and brushing your teeth. Use plants in your lawn that don't need a lot of water. And only water your lawn early or late in the day.

Pick up litter around rivers and lakes. Dirty water hurts animals. Dirty water can't be used by communities.

Turn off the lights when you're not using them. Power plants use water to make electricity. Power plants use less water if they don't have to make so much electricity. So use less electricity.

Eat less meat. Some animals are used as food for people. Animals need to drink water. Farms also use water to grow crops to feed these animals. If you eat less meat, fewer animals will be used as food. Less water will be used to raise them.

Check In Explain what is happening to the water in the Colorado River. Why does the river need to be saved?

GENRE Social Studies Article

Read to find out how different members of a river community worked together in an emergency.

Brace for

IT WAS THE AFTERNOON OF JANUARY 15, 2009.

The 155 passengers and crew members aboard U.S. Airways Flight 1549 fastened their seat belts. At 3:25 p.m., the plane took off from New York City. It was headed to Charlotte, North Carolina.

Two minutes after the plane left the ground, Eric Stevenson looked out the window. He was a passenger on the plane. He noticed a flock of geese flying next to the airplane. Seconds later he heard some knocking noises. He also smelled something burning.

At the plane's controls were Captain Chesley "Sully" Sullenberger and copilot Jeff Skiles. They knew that the plane had flown through a flock of geese. Some of the birds had been sucked into the engines. The plane had lost power.

Passengers make their way onto the plane's wings. They wait to be rescued from the middle of New York's Hudson River.

IMPACT

by Mattie Jaffe

Skiles tried to restart the engines, but nothing worked. There was no time to return to the airport. Captain Sullenberger would have to make an emergency landing. But where? Then he saw a wide, open space below them. It was the Hudson River. Landing there would be dangerous. But it was their only choice.

Captain Sullenberger made a calm announcement on the loudspeaker. He said, "Brace for impact." Passengers prepared themselves to hit the water.

Captain Sullenberger fell in love with flying and airplanes when he was a boy. Later, he became a pilot in the United States Air Force. As a pilot, Sully always put safety first. He also taught people how to fly planes safely. After the event on the Hudson River, Sully began working with the Young Eagles. That is a group that teaches children about airplanes.

A MIRACLE ON THE HUDSON

Not quite six minutes after takeoff, the huge plane dropped onto the Hudson River. All around were the tall buildings of New York City.

^ Emergency workers put on scuba gear so they can dive into the freezing water.

Pilot Sully knew just how to handle the plane. He didn't want it to flip over. He didn't want it to nosedive into the water. Sully landed the plane perfectly. His quick thinking saved everyone on board.

^ Firefighters throw a rope to passengers. The rope is used to secure the raft.

Landing the plane on the water also protected the people living and working in the city. Suppose the plane had gone down on the ground. Many more people's lives could have been in danger.

The **waterway** sprang to life at once. Rescue workers spotted passengers waiting on the plane's wings. Their boats sped from the shore to the plane. **Ferryboats**, which carry people back and forth across the wide river, raced toward the plane, too. The passengers could see that New Yorkers would rescue them quickly. They were wet and cold. But they were alive!

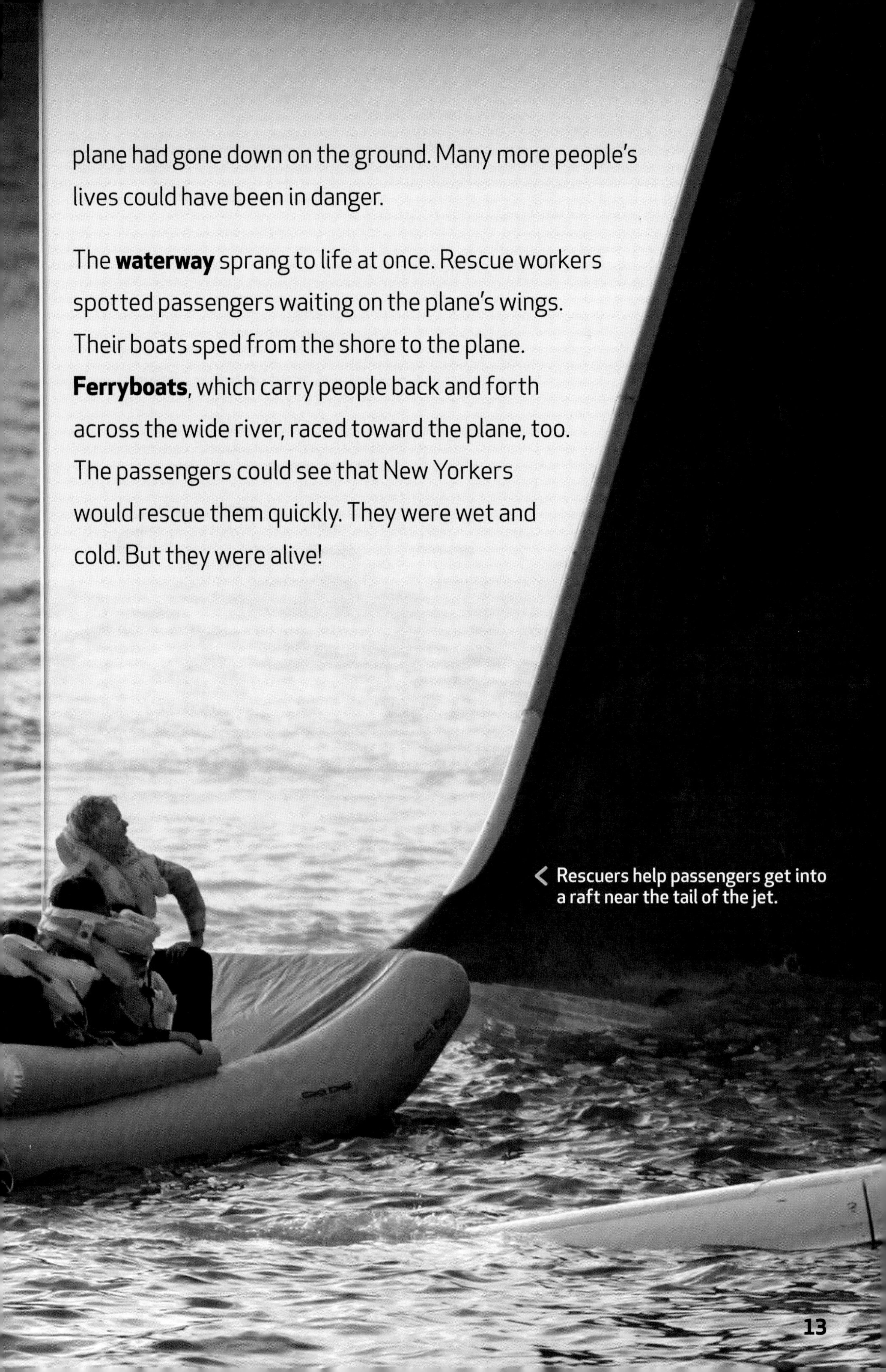

Rescuers help passengers get into a raft near the tail of the jet.

COMING TOGETHER

The boats picked up the passengers. They went to shore. Workers gave warm clothing to the tired, cold people.

People on land helped out, too. Restaurants fed hungry passengers. Nurses and doctors cared for the people who had been hurt. New Yorkers showed the passengers how much they cared.

People called Captain Sullenberger a hero. Sully just praised his crew. "I was very happy that everyone involved did their jobs extraordinarily well," he said.

Many different types of boats help in the rescue.

Check In What caused the plane to crash?

GENRE Opinion Piece

Read to find out about the pros and cons of living in New Orleans.

A City by

by Mattie Jaffe and Ann Wildman

Just Call Me "NOLA."

Listen. Can you hear the sound of a trumpet playing a tune? Breathe in. Do you smell fresh seafood gumbo? Do you see the riverboat splash by on the Mississippi River? You're in New Orleans, Louisiana. Some people call the city "NOLA" instead.

There is water on almost all sides of New Orleans. The city lies along the Mississippi River. Several lakes are nearby. So is the Gulf of Mexico. New Orleans has been a **port** since the 1700s. A port is a place on the water where ships load and unload goods. Around 6,000 ships travel along the Mississippi each year. They bring boxes of goods in

the Water

A look at New Orleans from across the Mississippi River

and out of New Orleans. These ships give many people jobs to do.

The people of New Orleans like to have fun along the water. But summers in New Orleans can be hot and steamy. Hurricanes, big storms with strong winds, sometimes strike during the fall. New Orleans can be a stormy place!

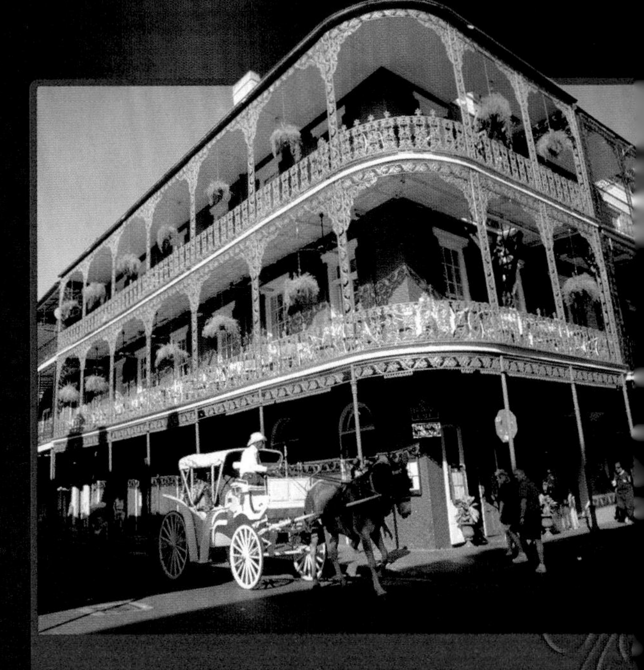

The French Quarter is a very old neighborhood in New Orleans. It is known for its historic buildings.

A Stormy City

In August 2005, weather experts watched a hurricane growing in the Gulf of Mexico. Would it hit New Orleans? On August 29, it did. The hurricane was named Katrina. Its strength surprised many people. Within hours, cars sank under rising floodwaters. Trees fell. Houses were destroyed. Many people had no electricity.

What caused all of this damage? Strong winds up to 170 miles-per-hour caused Gulf waters to rise. The rising water spilled over the **levee** walls. Levees had been built around New Orleans to protect the city from flooding. Everyone knew that a bad flood could hit New Orleans. They thought the levees would help. But Katrina was just too powerful.

> Hurricane Katrina caused 80 percent of New Orleans to flood.

Once the storm passed, help came. The American Red Cross, a group that helps people in need, provided meals and safe places to stay. Volunteer workers also helped families get clothing and groceries. Other helpers built safe homes for people whose homes were destroyed by Katrina.

It took several years, but New Orleans is strong again. Visitors have returned. They want to enjoy the things that make New Orleans special. The levees were also strengthened. People hope the levees will keep New Orleans safe the next time a storm hits.

Hurricane Katrina was the largest hurricane to hit the United States.

A volunteer saws lumber. He is helping rebuild a home near New Orleans.

Down on the Bayou

People in New Orleans love to spend time outdoors. Sometimes they visit the **bayou** (BY-oo). Bayous are marshy, slow-moving streams. There are many bayous near New Orleans.

Would you like to see a bayou? Sign up for a swamp tour! Hop aboard a boat. Maybe you will take a special boat called an airboat. Airboats are small boats with a large fan on the back. Air blasts through the fan to blow the boat across the water.

^ The bayous near New Orleans are home to many alligators.

v In the fall, some trees in the bayou turn orange.

Keep your eyes open. You'll see soft moss that seems to drip from tree branches. These mossy trees have strong roots that grow together. The roots form a wall below water. The root walls help keep floodwaters out of cities such as New Orleans.

In the bayou, the bugs fly around you like a thick cloud. There are lots of animals to see, too. Alligators live in the bayous. So do egrets. Egrets are large, beautiful wading birds. And don't miss the nutria. They look a little like beavers with long, rat-like tails. It's amazing that this wild setting is close to the city of New Orleans.

Let Loose

New Orleans is known for one of the biggest parties in the country. It is called Mardi Gras (MAHR-dee GRAH). This party happens before a holiday of fasting, or not eating certain foods. Mardi Gras is a chance for crowds to eat and have fun.

Some of the best parts of Mardi Gras are the parades. People wear fancy costumes and glittery masks. They hop on the floats and toss plastic coins to the crowd. These gifts are called "throws." Kids dress up in funny costumes hoping to get more throws. Throws are good luck.

Anyone can join special Mardi Gras parades called "second line parades." Musicians play **jazz** in these parades.

Jazz is a special type of music. It has a strong beat. Jazz music uses horns, drums, pianos, and other instruments. People hear this music as the parade walks by. They can join in the fun by dancing behind the musicians.

New Orleans is a city near the water. Sometimes it has storms and flooding. However, jazz, good food, parades, and bayou adventures make living in New Orleans exciting.

People spend all year building floats. Floats are made of wood and plaster.

Street bands lead dancers in a second line parade.

Check In Name one reason someone might want to live in New Orleans. Name one reason someone might not want to live there.

Discuss

1. What connects the three selections that you read in this book?
2. How do the communities along the Colorado River use the river's water? What are some ways communities such as yours can conserve water from rivers and lakes?
3. How did the water community of New York City work together to rescue the passengers of Flight 1549?
4. How does the location of New Orleans affect the people who live there?
5. What do you still wonder about living by the water?